CLAUS DALBY

CONTAINERS IN THE GARDEN

COOL
SPRINGS
PRESS

© 2022 Quarto Publishing Group USA Inc.
English translation © 2022 Quarto Publishing Group USA Inc.
Text and photography © 2022 Claus Dalby; except as noted otherwise

First Published in USA in 2022 by Cool Springs Press, an imprint of The Quarto Group, 100 Cummings Center, Suite 265-D, Beverly, MA 01915, USA.
T (978) 282-9590 F (978) 283-2742 Quarto.com

The original Danish edition was published as: Krukker i haven © Klematis A/S Denmark (www.klematis.dk)

Cool Springs Press titles are also available at discount for retail, wholesale, promotional, and bulk purchase. For details, contact the Special Sales Manager by email at specialsales@quarto.com or by mail at The Quarto Group, Attn: Special Sales Manager, 100 Cummings Center, Suite 265-D, Beverly, MA 01915, USA.

26 25 24 23 22   4 5

ISBN: 978-0-7603-7465-8

Digital edition published in 2022
eISBN: 978-0-7603-7466-5

Design: Claus Dalby
Cover Images: front cover Claus Dalby, back cover Nina Kestilä Hansen
Photography: Claus Dalby; except Christina Greve, pages 5, 13

Printed in China

Contents

Foreword

I have written a number of books on gardens, flowers, and decorations. It may sound odd that I can go on and on about plants, but I can. I love to communicate, especially in books.

Containers in the garden is a subject that I have worked on intensively over the years and continue to develop. That's why this is my fourth book on potted gardens.

There is a lot of interest, I sense, and this is certainly linked to the fact that it is a good place to start. For many, it can seem overwhelming to set out to building an entire garden. In contrast, it's a lot quicker and easier to plant some pots and arrange them. However, pots also require care. Watering, in particular, can be quite a challenge. So during vacations, you will have to enlist the help of friends or family.

Over time, I have become known for my passion for colors and my way of combining them. Naturally in the arrangement of flowers, but also very much in the use of foliage. They are great for creating breaks and for accentuating the flowers. Throughout the book I make a number of suggestions for plants whose foliage fits beautifully into a given color scheme. Often I feel like a fashion designer who is creating a collection that in many ways needs to fit together. It is my wish to pass on the knowledge and experience that I have acquired over many years.

Finally, I would like to thank you for the immense interest you have shown in my work on social media, where I regularly report on my life and work. It makes the process less lonely and it's nice to be reassured that you're on the right track.

A very big thank you also goes to my gardeners and other helpers, who are invaluable in my work.

Claus Dalby
clausdalby.com @clausdalby

My Containers

Almost all my pots are made of light terracotta clay, which takes patina well. Although these days there are many new materials that make the containers light and able to stand outside in winter, my favorite material is still clay. And let me be clear: there are no clay pots that are one hundred percent frost-proof! Some are more vulnerable than others; it depends on how hard they're fired. Hard-fired pots don't soak up as much water as pots fired at lower temperatures. And since it is the water that freezes and causes the pot to burst, extra care should be taken with pots that have been fired at lower temperatures.

In any case, the safest thing to do in autumn is to empty the clay pots of plants and potting soil and place them slightly raised above the ground with the bottom up. Then there is not much risk. Even better is to place the pots under a canopy, in a shed or perhaps a greenhouse.

If it is not possible to remove the soil because the plants will spend the winter in the pot, the danger of bursting is minimized by placing the pots under cover so that they do not get winter moisture.

If you use zinc or wooden containers, leaving them outside is not a problem. And the same is true for most fiber materials.

As for the look of the pots, it is of course a matter of taste, what you prefer. My taste has always been toward the unadorned and relatively stylish. If you look at the range in garden centers and nurseries, this is also the kind that is prominent today. In the past you could buy cheap glazed pots, often with carved motifs, but they seemed so strangely alien.

If you like pots and live by the motto that there is always room for one more, I can only recommend that you keep your eyes open. Not only when you are in the garden center or at the nursery, but also in the DIY store, department store, interior design store, second-hand shop, or at flea markets.

The Good Soil

It goes without saying that the soil in which plants grow must be of the best quality. Here, no expense shall be spared.

With soil, as with so much else, quality costs, so don't go for the cheapest product. After all, it's about plants thriving throughout the season, and they will only do so if the soil is of a quality that allows them to develop a good root network. You have to feel your way.

It may be possible to open a sack to check the soil: pick up a handful of potting soil and close your hand tightly around the soil. Then open your hand again. If the soil is compressed, it will not be suitable, but it also should not be so loose that it falls apart. An intermediate consistency is appropriate. When doing this little test, it is important that the bag has not been open so long that the soil has become dry. It should be slightly damp.

If the potting soil is easily compressed, it will naturally also form a large lump in the pot. This squeezes out the air, preventing oxygen from reaching the roots and causing the plant to die.

Another clue to the quality of the soil can be found by looking at the color. It should not be too dark, but not too light either. A nice chocolate brown color is usually a sign of quality. Good potting soil often contains vermiculite or perlite—small particles of expanded volcanic rocks that help to hold water and fertilizer. The soils' label will tell you whether the soil contains vermiculite or perlite.

For many years I was asked what kind of soil I used. But it was quite difficult to answer, because I used a professional grade that was not available to "ordinary" people. It was only for professional gardeners, yet I was lucky to get my hands on it.

Source a professional-grade potting soil that contains vermiculite or perlite. Ideally, it should also contain compost, composted cow manure, or another long-acting fertilizer—enough for a whole season. It's what makes the plants strut.

Plants from Seeds

Ever since I started taking an interest in gardening, I've loved propagating plants from seed. Even before the first seed catalogs arrive in the mail, I have to go online to see if the new selections have appeared on the various websites. It's always exciting to see what's new, and interesting things pop up every year. But the good old ones are not to be snuffed at either. There are plants that I have in my rotation every year.

You can buy a lot of plants, and I do, but it's really special to grow them yourself. For me, one of the most essential things about gardening is sowing a seed and watching it sprout and grow. It's basic and fundamental and I think it speaks to our primordial brain.

Another joy of seed propagation, of course, is that you can grow many plants that aren't available commercially. There is so much to choose from.

There is a big difference in how long it takes for a seed to develop into a flowering plant. For some it's quite quick—eight to ten weeks. These are the annual plants that can be sown directly at the growing site. That's why they're called hardy. If you're buying seeds, it's handy to know that this group is called Hardy Annuals—in seed catalogs sometimes abbreviated HA.

Which flowers belong in the hardy category? Roughly speaking, many of them are found in bags of mixed summer flowers. They are so easy that even a five year old can grow them in his own garden. They include larkspur, field poppies, calendula, forget-me-nots, black-eyed Susans, and bachelor buttons. These seeds can be sown directly in pots and later thinned if they are too dense. You can also sow in trays and transplant as explained on the following page.

If you're serious about growing plants from seed, the Half-Hardy Annuals (HHA) are an exciting challenge. Plants in this group take so long to develop from seed that they need a head start indoors (pre-cultivation) and are often sown in the late winter or early spring.

I am aware that some people have a bad experience with starting seeds indoors because the plants easily become long and unwieldy and almost impossible to handle. But it is not that difficult: It's all about light versus heat. When the seeds are sown, light is lacking. Although the small plants are placed under a bright window sill, there is not enough light to match the indoor temperature. Therefore, plants must be given supplementary electric light.

First, the seeds must be sown in trays, and it is convenient if the trays are not very large. The bottom of milk cartons, empty plastic food storage containers and the like are a suitable size. Remember to make holes in the bottom. Fill with seed starting mix, which is a lightweight potting soil with sparse nutrients/fertilizer. If there are too many nutrients in the soil, there is a risk that the roots will be burned and the plants will die out.

Water and wait a few hours for the soil to settle. Then sprinkle the seeds evenly and cover them lightly, preferably with vermiculite. Generally speaking, smaller seeds should be covered only slightly and larger ones correspondingly more.

Some seeds are light-sprouting. This means that they only germinate if they get light—they do not have to be covered. If this is the case, it will usually be on the seed packet. This may also include other relevant information, so it pays to read the seed packet's "How To Guide" before getting started.

Place a loose layer of thin plastic over the trays and store indoors at 68–72°F (20–22°C). Now check on them at least once a day, and when the first green sprouts appear, move the plants to a light windowsill in a room with temperature about 59°F (15°C).

Each time the seedlings are watered, let them draw water from below. Pour the water into a tray or similar, so that it reaches about halfway up the seed trays. After half an hour, take the trays out again; now the soil has drawn the water it needs. This is repeated every four or five days.

Watering from below keeps the top layer of soil from becoming too wet which often results in plants being attacked by root rot. This causes the stems to rot and the plants to collapse. Then they are beyond saving.

Within two or three weeks, the plants have developed their first true leaves and are then transplanted into trays or pots. The small plants are gently lifted out of the soil. It is important to be very gentle so that the roots are not damaged more than is absolutely necessary. The plants are handled with two fingers around one of the leaves, which is the least vulnerable on the plant.

Nutrient-enriched potting soil is filled into pots or trays with compartments. Holes are made in the soil with a dowel or pencil. The plants are carefully inserted into the holes and the soil is lightly compacted around them. For the first few days, the plants need to get used to their new surroundings, but then they really take off. Moving into the nutrient-rich soil really suits them. From this point on they will grow fast.

If you have a greenhouse, the plants can be moved out in the mid-spring. If it gets below 50°F (10°C), you'll need to keep a small heater on. And when the plants have gotten used to the outdoors after a good week, you can just turn on the heater if it gets below 41°F (5°C).

The secret is to give the plants enough light as they grow. In reality, It's nothing extraordinary—you just have to imitate nature.

When the plants have grown nicely enough in size, they are planted in pots.

Bulbs in Pots

Growing bulbs in pots is beautiful and effective, and not difficult if you take a few simple precautions.

The timing of the planting depends on whether they are spring or summer flowering bulbs.

The most common spring bulbs—daffodils, hyacinths, and tulips—are planted in the fall. It is particularly important that narcissus bulbs are planted in early fall because they need time to form a good root network. The others can wait until later in the autumn. To tell the truth, we occasionally have had so much trouble getting everything ready that we have even planted bulbs in December.

Put 2–4 inches (5–10 cm) of pebbles in the pot, and then fill it about halfway with potting soil. The amount of potting soil is adjusted so that the bulbs can be placed at a depth of three times their height. Fill up with potting soil. Finally, water well. Then water only in spring, when the green appears above the soil.

Once the bulbs are planted, place the pots in a protected spot. This could be an outbuilding, a garage or under a plastic cover. The bulbs do not need light during the cold months, but they must be protected against winter rot. If the bulbs are kept too wet, they will rot and, by their very nature, no flowers will appear. They can cope with frost.

It is recommended to check the pots during the winter, because bulbs have one enemy in particular, and that is rodents like mice, chipmunks, and voles. That's why we always cover the potted bulbs with hardware screening before putting the pots into winter storage.

In early spring, when the sprouts appear above the soil, it's time to put the pots out in the open. Only now should you start watering.

Then it's just a matter of waiting—until the daffodils and hyacinths burst forth and the tulips soon after. A tip to speed up flowering is to put some of the pots in the greenhouse. That way you can get flowers about two weeks earlier. When the buds are about to burst, move the pots outside.

Summer-flowering bulbs, such as gladiolus and lilies, are planted in exactly the same way as spring-flowering bulbs, but not until mid-spring. The first to start flowering are the lilies, which flower around July, while the gladioli wait until late August.

Dahlias in Pots

Dahlias are one of my absolute favorite flowers in late summer. No other plant offers a richness of flowers like dahlias.

Dahlias need plenty of sun; otherwise they don't bloom at all. In my beds there is no room for dahlias because the perennials fill the beds up completely. Instead, I grow dahlias in pots—several hundred of them.

As most people will know, dahlias are tuberous and it is important that the pot is not too small. It should be half to a full size larger than a mop bucket. We put three tubers in each pot in April. As with bulbs, put 2–4 inches (5–10 cm) of pebbles in the pot. Then fill in the soil, leaving about 4 inches (10 cm) up to the edge. The tubers are placed in the pot and covered up with a few inches of soil, which is watered well. If frost is expected, the pots are covered. When the plants are about 20 inches (half a meter) tall, we support them with stands as shown on the next page. Remember to fertilize thoroughly throughout the summer.

Planting

Before putting soil in any pot, make sure there are enough holes in the bottom for the water to drain. If not, carefully drill them out.

Next, fill the pot about a fifth full pebbles to form a good drainage layer. Add the soil and press it lightly so that, depending on the size of the plants, there are 6–8 inches (15–20 cm) free up to the edge. Finally, water the container thoroughly. The plant(s) must also be well watered when they move to the pot. Therefore, water them carefully four or five hours before planting.

Place the plants in the pot and fill with soil, leaving about 2 inches (5 cm) to the rim. This makes watering easier. Water one last time.

Now the plants need some time to settle in, so it's a good idea to put them in partial shade for the first week. After that, they can be moved to full sun, provided they are sun-loving plants.

It is said that summer plants are sold four times during a season. The first time is at winter's end, when the whole family gets a feeling of spring and goes shopping for their garden beds and containers. The second time is around the date of your last spring frost because the first flowers have died after the cold shock inflicted on them by early planting. The third time is at the end of July, when many come home from vacation to find the pot plants dead from lack of water. And fourthly and finally in late summer or early fall, when summer plants start to look a little sad and can be successfully replaced by late summer plants such as chrysanthemums, asters and ornamental cabbages.

An old rule says that summer flowers must not be planted in the garden beds before the danger of frost has passed. Only after that date is there any certainty that the cold temperatures are over. With the above rule in mind, there is no need to rush to plant geraniums and other delicate summer flowers. It doesn't take much imagination to visualize what happens when a flower that has been in a warm greenhouse for the previous months is suddenly exposed to cold weather.

The only things you can plant out in pots in the early spring with reasonable certainty are pansies or violets and bellis that won't succumb to a few degrees of frost. They may look a bit soggy and worn, but they'll soon rise again.

Water and Fertilizer

All plants need water to thrive. Some will outright die, or fail badly, if they dry out just once. This is true of roses, for example.

Therefore, before purchasing too many pots, it is important to make sure that you have time to water them. If you are planting in unglazed pots, on hot days you should go out with the watering can or hose once or twice a day. The rapid evaporation in the porous clay pots can be remedied a bit by covering the inside with plastic before the soil is added—remember to poke holes in the bottom! If you use containers made of zinc or iron, you will find that they are somewhat better at holding water.

When watering, don't just lightly sprinkle. At least a couple of times during the week, the soil in the pot needs to be watered completely, and not all at once. Here it is important to return with the watering can or hose two or three times at intervals of a few minutes. If you have many pots, you have to water with a hose. It's simply too time-consuming with a watering can. A hose with a watering wand makes the job relatively simple. With a little dexterity, you can clean the plants of wilted flowers with one hand while watering with the other.

I am often asked if we have an automatic watering system. The answer is "no."
We water the good old-fashioned way.

Plants do not live on water alone, but also need to be fertilized. For the first three or four weeks, however, it is not necessary to think about nutrition, because the fresh potting soil contains enough fertilizer for a little over a month. But after that, the ration is used up and you have to do it yourself.

There are many options for adding fertilizer. One of them is to give the plants liquid fertilizer when watering. Of course, this method requires watering with a watering can.

If you want to make it easy, you can use a long-acting fertilizer in granular form. They provide plants with the right nutrition for five or six months, and the fertilizer is released as the weather warms up.

Perennials in Pots

If you have the opportunity to store the plants in winter, you can enjoy the same plants year after year. Even some of the summer flowers we think of as annuals can actually come back if they are kept frost-free. This is the case for daisies, flowering tobacco, and petunias. One question, of course, is whether you want the inconvenience of bringing plants like these through the winter. They don't cost that much, but it's nice.

When I talk about winter storage, I mostly think about different types of plant covers, because most people don't have a heated greenhouse. But many plants can actually withstand frost. This is true of almost all perennials; at least the ones we plant in our gardens. If they're in a pot, however, they don't like to be too wet in winter. In the cold and dark months, the plants are in a dormant state and the amount of water they need is limited. In fact, too much water can be fatal.

If a pot of plants is left uncovered in winter, the plants can soon start to rot. When it freezes, a plug forms at the bottom of the pot, preventing water from draining away. And then the plant is at risk of dying because the roots can't get air. Therefore, the pots need some kind of cover. This could be in a garage, shed, greenhouse, or similar. If you can offer them that, there are many perennials, climbers, shrubs, and small trees that do well in pots. Some of the most obvious perennials are hosta, daisies, coneflowers, sages, and other flower and foliage plants.

To help perennials thrive, it is recommended to give them fresh soil and possibly a larger pot every spring. Carefully remove the plant from the pot and remove one to two thirds of the soil with your fingers. Then pot the plant again and water well. This transplanting helps to nourish the roots and thus the plant. Some perennials, for example hosta, can be difficult to get out of the pot. In that case, you just have to renew the top layer of soil and otherwise spoil the plant with fertilizer. At some point, however, the roots will burst the pot and the plant will obviously need a larger container.

Change of Scene

The idea behind this book is to illustrate how to keep the flower display going throughout the season—from spring to winter. This section shows how the scenery changes as the weather gets warmer and nature turns green.

The picture above was taken in mid-April, and the next page shows how it all looked three weeks later. The color scheme is the same—white and yellow. In April there is a predominance of yellow, and later the whites and creams take over. At first it's the daffodils that dominate, and then later the tulips.

The pots of daffodils are arranged outside the gate at the beginning of April. At that time there are only buds; the only things showing color are white and pale-yellow violets and bellis.

The tulip pots seen on the next page are stored behind the house and as the daffodils finish blooming, they will be replaced. In this way there is always something going on.

One of the questions I am often asked is what we do with the bulbs after flowering. After the daffodils flower, we lift the soil and plants out of the pots, which is quite easy to do because the roots hold it all together. You can also just leave the pots untouched,

but we want to be able to plant new plants in them. The daffodil stems and leaves need time to wither completely. When the stems let go of the soil with a gentle tug, you can pull out the bulbs and leave them sitting out to dry for the summer. In autumn they are planted again.

You can do the same with tulips. However, it should be noted that depending on the variety, there is a big difference in how many bulbs are able to flower the following year. I take no chances, so here the tulip bulbs end up in the compost.

Not only outside the gate, but also in many places around the garden we have large groups of spring bulbs in pots. See for example the picture on the next page. Here too the color scheme is white and yellow.

Color Joy

Working with color has always been my passion. We lived in a lot of places before we moved here. Back then, it was the houses and not the gardens that interested me.

For the first six months in the new house, I used my love of color to decorate a red, a yellow, and an orange living room—en suite. Then my interest in gardens was awakened, and now I work on decorating and coloring the outdoors.

For a long time, both indoors and out, I worked in monochrome—tone on tone—but at some point I became more daring and colorful, especially when it came to the pot arrangements. I started combining colors like pink, purple, orange, blue, and lime. It was something that appealed to me and my followers, so I embraced that tonal range, but not just when it comes to tulips. I also mix dahlias, summer flowers, and perennials together.

Key players in my colorful tulip arrangements include the fringed tulip 'Cuban Night' above. Also pink 'Barcelona,' purple 'Paul Scherer,' and orange 'Ballerina.' The photo on pages 30–31 shows the purple 'Blue Diamond' at the top left between orange tulips, and to the right of that the purple 'Recreado.' The pansy is called 'Frizzle Sizzle Blue.'

Glowing Spring

Many people associate glowing tones—orange, for example—with autumn, but I like to turn things around. Orange and red are not typical spring tones, but it seems they have become more "accepted" in the last few years. I can tell from comments on pictures I post on social media. Until a few years ago, I often showed orange spring flowers, and several people wrote that they thought the color belonged in autumn. Since then, that has changed. Now orange is at the forefront of garden fashion.

There are two spring flowers I have a hard time gardening without. They are the violet and the primrose. The latter comes in a rich variety and I am particularly fond of the long-stemmed one, *Primula veris*. It's so pretty in pots, where I often plant three to five together, depending on the size of the pot. Here they stay nice for a few weeks. Then they are planted out in the garden beds, where they come back year after year.

The pictures also show two plants that are not common pot plants. They are both spurges. The tall slender grayish one is the spurge, *Euphorbia lathyris*, which we grow from seed. With its peculiar shape it is suitable in many contexts. The flowers are nothing special—small and yellowish, but the seeds are quite decorative. Another perennial spurge is the dark-leaved *Euphorbia amygdaloides* 'Purpurea,' which is beautiful in several stages. In the photo at the bottom right you can see how fine the foliage is and you can also sense the lime-shaped buds are about to pop out.

The pictures on this page are from late March, and the following pages show how the dark-leaved spurge is evolving from being a relatively inconspicuous player to playing an important role with its distinctive flowers.

Citrus and Daffodils

It is often chance that determines what I plant and combine in my pots. It depends on what I have and what I come across at nurseries and garden centers. Thus, I have not previously used citrus fruits as part of my potting arrangements. But when I happened to come across some nice kumquat plants, *Fortunella margarita*, I was inspired to include them in a display on the stairs. I also reused the orange primroses and violets seen on the previous page. The dark-leaved anemones are also repeat visitors. In addition, I had some daffodils—'Geranium'—in stock, and with their orange centers they were perfect.

Kumquat is quite easy to deal with. It's a great starter citrus fruit if you take a few simple precautions. First of all, citrus fruits should be watered with distilled water. In winter, the plants are kept frost-free at a maximum of 50°F (10°C). From March/April they can withstand temperatures of 59–68°F (15–20°C). It is at this time that the white flowers burst forth and emit the most delightful fragrance. Later, fruits begin to develop.

Tulips in Focus

In early May, the tulips in pots move to permanent locations in the garden. They haven't really shown color yet, but in a few weeks they will be in full bloom. Here are the two familiar orange varieties: the semi-full 'Princess Irene' and the tall and slender lily-shaped 'Ballerina.'

The dark-leaved *Euphorbia amygdaloides* 'Purpurea' has unfolded its flowers and attracts with its peculiar, attention-grabbing lime green color. They stay beautiful for a month or so, and then we cut the plants right down to the ground. It is worth mentioning here that the milky white juice of the stalks is poisonous. It is therefore important to wear gloves and wash your hands thoroughly after handling.

In just a few weeks, the spurges sprout again and come out with fresh foliage. This time, however, somewhat greener than the first time. Kumquat and violet still play along, and occasionally a new player is seen, namely the ninebark, *Physocarpus opulifolius* 'Lady in Red,' with almost copper-colored foliage. It is very good in many contexts. During the season it generates a lot of slender, straight growth. Just cut it back a bit, and new and fresh shoots appear.

In the background, *Euphorbia lathyris*—now with its round green seeds.

Inspiration

I am often asked, "What inspires you when putting together plants and flowers?" It's not so easy to answer unequivocally, but I am certainly drenched in inspiration all the time: When I'm on social media, when I'm travelling and generally moving around. Looking back at what I've created over the years purely in terms of gardening, it's clear that things have evolved in line with fashion, the environment, and supply.

It can be a single flower or plant that sets something in motion. This was the case here, for example, where I started with the two-tone tulip 'Abu Hassan.' I probably wouldn't have chosen it years ago, when I was more drawn to the pink, purple and violet varieties. The "safe" ones you could call them.

I was lucky enough to find a few trays of pansies whose tones almost echoed 'Abu Hassan.' They were planted in pots, and then I went hunting among the other plants in my stash. The fine red oxalis with green eye, *Trifolium repens* 'Isabella,' is a regular every year.

The large picture also shows the dark-leaved ninebark, *Physocarpus opulifolius* 'Diabolo.' At the back is a dark-leaved Japanese maple, *Acer japonicum* 'Sumi Nagashi.' Japanese maple features in several of my pot arrangements because it is slow-growing and never gets too vigorous.

As you can see from many of the pictures in the book, I often arrange containers on stairs, which we have a lot of. This way the plants are beautifully presented.

It Looks Black …

Plants with dark foliage and dark flowers have always been attractive. And that's what I've taken advantage of on the steps by the garden room. Here, it's very much the dark tulips—'Continental,' 'Black Hero,' and 'Queen of Night'—that command attention. But without the accompaniment of various foliage plants, the experience would not be the same.

There are some so-called black tulips. 'Vincent van Gogh,' 'Black Parrot,' 'Negrita,' 'Cafe Noir,' and 'Cuban Night' must also be mentioned here. However, it should be said that there are no tulips with completely black flowers—they are all almost burgundy. In addition, they have different flowers and are of varying height.

The best known of all dark tulips is the 'Queen of Night,' which with its slender graceful stems is always noticed in the garden. It's a fairly faithful variety that's good at coming back. When planting in containers, however, be aware that 'Queen of Night' grows quite tall and tends to topple over.

The tall dark Japanese maple against the wall is called 'Sumi Nagashi,' and the somewhat lower red one is called 'Beni Maiko.'

Rex begonia, *Begonia rex* is a well-known pot plant. At one point it seemed to go out of fashion, and as demand declined, many gardeners removed it from their collection.

Today it has regained its honor and dignity, and the supply is quite large. Not only are the colors of the foliage impressive, but so are the leaf patterns. Sometimes you see leaves that are even snail-shell shaped. Not so long ago an elderly gardener told me that they also call begonias "bias leaf." This is because no leaf is symmetrical.

The rex begonia is propagated by leaf cuttings: the stem is cut off very close to the leaf. The leaf is then cut into postage stamp-sized pieces, placed on top of damp potting soil in a tray and pressed lightly into the soil. In a few weeks, small plants will grow from the leaf veins. To encourage root formation, the edges of the leaf pieces can be dipped in rooting hormone powder, available from the nursery. A plastic bag is then pulled over the tray to maintain even humidity. To prevent the cuttings from rotting in too much moisture, it is a good idea to cut a corner off the bag.

When the small new plants are big enough to handle, they are planted into individual pots of nutrient-enriched soil, where they will quickly grow.

Bellis and Primroses

Two plants that are firmly in my spring repertoire are bellis and primula. They can withstand some freezing temperatures. Sure, they are toppled by frost, but as soon as the temperature rises above freezing, they rise again. However, if it gets colder than 23°F (-5°C), it's a good idea to cover them with a piece of fabric, a row cover, or similar.

Already between Christmas and New Year, the colorful primroses appear in the shops. Out with the Christmas decorations and in with Spring! I think that's how a lot of us feel. These very early primroses are for indoor use only, and they won't survive in garden beds, even if you wait until spring to plant them out.

The range of bellis is not that large. There are only three colors—white, pink and burgundy. However, the flowers vary somewhat depending on the variety. I swear by the 'Tasso' series with button-like flowers. Pictured here is 'Tasso White.' The pink one, which I can't live without either, is called 'Tasso Strawberries and Cream.'

Note also the variegated ivy, which I use in a number of contexts.

Tulips in Good Company

The photos on the previous page are from late March, while the photos here were taken about a month later. I rearranged them a few weeks earlier, when the tulips in the pots started to show buds. Then the tulips opened and became part of the parade. The variety is called 'Ivory Floradale.'

In addition to bellis, primroses, and tulips, I have supplemented with moonlight yellow pansies—'Delta Primrose.' But if the choice is between pansies and violets, *Viola cornuta*, the latter wins. There is a lot of care with pansies because they have to be deadheaded all the time to keep looking good. The violets don't need to be nipped at all and keep looking nice for a few months. After that, they can get a little too wild. Then we take a pair of scissors and cut the plants—flowers, leaves and stems—down to about half height and give them a dab of fertilizer. In a couple of weeks they start to resprout and a good month later they are in full bloom again.

To add height to the arrangement, I have also included *Physocarpus opulifolius* 'Darts Gold,' with lime-yellow foliage. The same shade of color is given by the mockorange, *Philadelphus coronarius* 'Aureus,' seen in front of the tulips.

The White Garden

There is something beautiful and very clean about white gardens—a style that appeals to many. My garden consists of about fifteen garden rooms, several of which are devoted to the white color scheme. But the mood can also be transferred to potted arrangements.

The term "white garden" is closely associated with England and the Sissinghurst Castle Garden, where Vita Sackville-West (1892–1962) and Harold Nicolson (1886–1968) created the most beautiful garden spaces and masterfully composed plants in the most sublime way. Thus, from 1949, they created The White Garden with exclusively white flowers and gray-leaved plants. Today it is one of the most iconic gardens in Europe.

The gray foliage is an important player along with the white flowers. The flowers play the main role, while the silver foliage has an important extra role. Without it, the expression would be much less elegant.

The gray lobed plant at the top right is useful in many contexts. Dusty Miller, *Cineraria maritima* 'Silver Dust,' is its name. Not many other silver-gray plants are as easy to deal with as this one. Firstly, Dusty Miller is easy to propagate from seed, and secondly, it only gets more beautiful throughout the season as it grows.

Below is the Texas sage, *Salvia farinacea* 'Cirrus White,' which meets both conditions with gray foliage and white flowers. It doesn't make much of a fuss.

Hostas are also fine. It is one of the most grateful pot plants there is. Every three or four years they are replanted—when they are outgrowing the pot. Throughout the summer they receive liquid fertilizer.

Hosta 'Francee'—top left of previous page—has green leaves with a white margin that lights up between the white and gray. Another nice hosta is the gray 'Halcyon,' seen on the bottom right. When it comes to white summer flowers, there are a lot to choose from. But I still make sure to limit myself. It's better to have a few varieties in repeated groups than many different ones.

Nemesia, *Nemesia fruticans* 'Karoo White'—top of previous page—has small white flowers that last all summer. It is a bred variety that needs to be propagated by cuttings. The same goes for the white *Verbena* 'Lanai Blush White' at the bottom left. If you remove withered inflorescences throughout the season, the flowering will continue.

Earlier I explained how to revive violets, *Viola cornuta*, by cutting them halfway down after the first flowering. This is exactly how we treated the violets above in mid-May. And when this picture was taken at the end of June, they looked fine and fresh again. This is definitely a second youth.

We often think of the violet primarily as a spring flower, but if you visit a nursery in the autumn, you will find that both pansies and violets are also available for fall planting.

In late August, a few months after the photos on pages 46–49 were taken, it was time for a refresh. The Hosta, Dusty Miller, and *Verbena* held up. The photo on pages 50–51 shows what has taken over: Bottom from left are heather, cushion bush, roses, *Helichrysum petiolare*, budded chrysanthemum balls, ornamental cabbage, and wire vine.

On the second step, a gray-leaved *Sedum*—'Blue Cushion'—is seen between the wire vine and heather. Above is the gray-leaved kale 'Nero di Toscana.'

Above is a section of the picture on the previous page with cabbage as the center. The beauty of the cabbage plant is that it is both gray and white, unifying the tones of the arrangement. Here, the cabbage plant plays the lead role, while the wire vine plant is a clear extra. It is good in most combinations.

Under the windows of the garden room are long boxes, which are always planted with white flowers and grayish growths.

This year it was white daisies accompanied by silver falls, *Dichondra argentea*, and cushion bush, *Calocephalus brownii*.

The Sunken Garden

Of the garden's many different spaces, The Sunken Garden is one that garden guests particularly notice. This is probably because the large open space forms a restful space in the otherwise experience-saturated garden. The use of white and greenish flowers, together with predominantly gray foliage, is also an attractive feature.

All the plants are planted in pots, and as you can see from the pictures, I work very much with symmetry. The large picture on the previous pages shows how I use different pots. The two zinc boxes are called Versailles boxes and in them are planted hydrangea 'Little Lime.'

Next to the Versailles boxes are two large, checkered sandstone pots—Elizabethan Jardinière—from Haddonstone in England. As mentioned, everything in and around this room is planted in pots and planter boxes. The only exceptions are the umbrella-shaped oak trees.

The white inflorescences sticking up on either side of the center are *Hydrangea paniculata* 'Silver Dollar.' As is clear from the photo on pages 64–65, the shrubs are upright.

From the garden room, seen on the right of the picture, I have a clear view of The Sunken Garden. This is where I have my office and spend many hours.

The garden room was designed by garden and landscape architect Kjeld Slot, with whom I am in constant dialogue. It's so rewarding to have a good sparring partner—in the same way as when you start building a house. I don't know anyone here who hasn't already consulted an architect. So my best advice to new garden owners is to seek professional help if you want more than just a lawn with beds around it.

Initially Kjeld Slot suggested hedge-lined parterre rows, but as I wanted the whole space to be planted exclusively with potted plants, I opted instead for angular hedges. They made it more flexible to move and place the pots.

We also discussed the framing of the room, and here the choice fell on a low rooftop hedge and trained hornbeams, as I had so often seen in Holland and for many years had desired.

The Grays

There are so many foliages in a myriad of varying tones. I've already mentioned several, but here are a good handful more of the grays.

Above is the moth plant, *Plectranthus argentea* 'Silver Shield,' which with its velvety leaves is a plant I cherish. The thing is, moth plants don't tolerate frost, but need to be kept at least 41°F (5°C), preferably warmer, over the winter. It can survive winters indoors in a cold but bright windowsill. Many years ago I bought a plant in England and have since taken hundreds of cuttings—partly for my own use and partly for friends and acquaintances.

One year I was unfortunate enough to lose my mother plants because we didn't get them moved in before frost. So I searched online for a plant that I could take cuttings from, but to no avail. However, I came across an English company selling seeds. This surprised me, because I did not know that moth plants could be propagated from seed. It had to be tried, and soon I had a stock again.

Siberian bugloss, *Brunnera macrophylla*, is an old perennial that also looks good in pots. This species has green leaves and blue forget-me-not-like flowers. A few years ago a new variety appeared with beautiful silver leaves and blue flowers; 'Jack Frost' is its name. Later came 'Betty Bowring,' which offers foliage identical to 'Jack Frost,' but has white flowers. They match the silver foliage very well. After flowering we cut the plants all the way down—both leaves and flower stems. This means that a few weeks later they will have a new set of leaves that will stay nice for the rest of the season.

Blue star fern, *Phlebodium aureum* 'Blue Star,' is a potted plant that has become widespread in recent years because of its beautiful blue-dusted foliage.

It does well outdoors throughout the summer in a semiprotected space.

When you have several hundred—or maybe more like several thousand—different plants, it's very interesting that it's often the same handful that guests notice when they see the garden. Showstoppers is what my garden mentor, Anne Just, called this phenomenon.

One plant that a lot of people ask me about is silver sage, *Salvia argentea*. Several people think it is a variety of lamb's ear, *Stachys byzantina*, with extra large leaves. This is due to the hairy foliage, which is actually even more downy than the lamb's ear. But it is a sage grown from seed. For the plants to reach a size like this, where three are planted together, they have to be sown quite early, preferably in early March. Later in the season, white flowers appear in warm summers. But it is the foliage that is the main attraction. Silver sage is a fairly short-lived plant that can be difficult to get through winters. It is important that the soil is not too moist.

Another remarkable plant that has gradually become widespread is *Euphorbia* 'Diamond Frost' with tiny white flowers. You can't propagate it yourself, and it's also hard to overwinter. This is because it requires a lot of heat. Summers that are cool and rainy mean that 'Diamond Frost' will not produce the "fizz" it is known for in warm summers.

Wire vine, *Muehlenbeckia*, is not only a nice indoor pot plant. It thrives outdoors and even tolerates a little frost. In fact, many of the plants we have indoors do even better outdoors. With foliage plants, however, be aware that most like to be in light partial shade.

Play with Foliage

Once you realize how many different types of foliage there are, a whole new world opens up. The plant pictured above was completely new to me when I saw it at a German garden show. It was a real showstopper with its velvety, almost white leaves. A sign revealed the name: *Senecio candicens* 'Angel Wings.' I got plants from Holland and they lit up the whole summer. A new love ...

The next page shows a number of plants with variegated foliage. They are all important players in my white garden. Sometimes I hear gardeners say they don't like variegated foliage. I don't feel that way—on the contrary. If you don't overdo the use, they can be very elegant.

The white-striped reed grass, *Phalaris arundinacea* 'Picta,' is fine, but it is invasive and spreads quickly in the bed, soon becoming a nuisance. In pots you don't have that problem. Another good pot plant is hosta, as mentioned, and there are countless beautiful varieties. In the picture to the right is *Hosta crispula*.

At the bottom is tatarian dogwood, *Cornus alba* 'Elegantissima'—a decorative shrub. Finally—on the right—is the lungwort, *Pulmonaria longifolia* 'Diana Clare.'

I've always had a fondness for green flowers, and one that we sow every spring is love-lies-bleeding, *Amaranthus caudatus* 'Emerald Tassels.' You don't often see this green variety. The purple one (see page 143) is more common. There is also a golden one, see page 110.

To allow the plants to develop, I sow them in March/April. Plant them in a tray, preferably in a greenhouse, and when the seedlings are big enough to handle, transplant them directly into pots.

Stonecrop, *Sedum spectabile*, is one of the best known and easiest perennials both in bed and pot. It requires virtually no care—no watering and no fertilizing, or it will grow long and lanky. For the same reason, it should not be replanted either.

At the end of the season, rose to pink flowers appear, but it's not because of them that I really like stonecrop. In fact, I like the green buds much more. To prevent the plants from flowering too early, we cut them halfway down around midsummer. Shortly afterward the plants start to sprout again and soon after the buds appear.

Grasses are good in many contexts, and there are countless different species and varieties. One of the easiest is the blue lyme grass, *Leymus arenarius* 'Blue Dune.' With its blue-dusted spikes, it's perfect for the white garden.

It almost goes without saying why this garden room is dubbed The Sunken Garden. The reason, of course, is that it was built below ground level. The pots are close together, almost forming small beds that are largely symmetrical. However, the fact that the arrangements are not completely perfect adds something to the composition. Minor deviations help to give life.

We first arrange the groups in a completely symmetrical way, and then we switch them around a bit.

As I said, plants and pots look particularly good on a staircase. There's plenty of opportunity for that here, where the space is just 3 feet (1 m) below ground level. The paving is old cobblestones, which are used in many places in the garden. Characteristic of The Sunken Garden are the straight lines, which are not only seen in the design of the room, but also in the hedges, trees, and pond. I am a proponent of rigor in garden design, where plants and flowers themselves contribute organic forms.

Late Season Touches

To conclude the description of my white pot arrangements, here are examples of plants that cope well with some cold. In fact, these photos were taken in early November. However, if more than a few degrees of night frost are forecast, I recommend covering the plants with a row cover, fabric, or similar.

The evergreen plant in the middle of the picture on the left is called *Skimmia japonica*. Note that it is a small shrub and therefore needs to be planted in a heavier potting soil, perhaps with pine bark chunks added, instead of the usual potting soil. *Skimmia* is a hungry plant that needs a lot of fertilizer to maintain its beautiful green foliage. It will do well in a pot for a few seasons, just be careful not to get it too damp. If at any point it starts to look a bit dull, it's time to plant it out in the garden. If the garden soil is alkaline, dig a large hole first and add some peat moss.

In front is the beautiful blue dusted foliage of the Christmas Rose, *Helleborus niger*. The small, low growth with white berries is wintergreen, *Gaultheria miqueliana*. It too is a small shrub. Finally, white ornamental cabbage is seen in the photo to the right. They light up so nicely in an arrangement like this.

I bought the moss-like *Selaginella apoda* in the checkered concrete pot in the front row at *Copenhagen Markets* in the spring. It will be interesting to see if I can get it through the winter in one piece. I'll put it in the heated greenhouse, and we'll see. In many cases, it's not just about temperature, but also moisture. My bet is that it will only need sparce watering through the winter.

Behind the *Selanginella* is the coralbell Heuchera 'Lime Rickey,' and to the right of it the Japanese sedge *Carex oshimensis* 'Evergold.' It's a charming little plant that blends so well with the other lime yellow foliage. 'Evergold' is evergreen and tolerates some freezing temperatures, but the foliage can get a bit dull over winter. Then you can cut the plant back and let it grow again. However, growth is not always so harmonious after this operation. That's why we overwinter our plants in the greenhouse.

I have also planted heather and ivy. At the far end is *Eucalyptus*, and to the left of the door is *Choisya* 'Aztec Gold.' In spring it is almost bright lime yellow.

Creme de la Creme

There are many plants with cream-colored flowers, and I often combine them with cool yellow tones. Not just flowers, but foliage too. Similar to plants with gray foliage, there is also a wide range of plants with lime yellow tones. And I am a lover of most of them. I'm so happy with my angel trumpets, *Brugmansia*. Not only because they create stature, but also because they have the amazing quality of being fragrant. Absolutely fabulous… especially in the evening.

It's impressive to see how much an angel trumpet grows in a single season. It can easily grow up to 3 feet (1 m) in height. That's why we prune the trees before moving them into the heated greenhouse, before the frost. Here they stand at 41–50°F (5–10°C) throughout the winter.

Short-statured dahlias are easy to fit into an arrangement. Here are a few—on either side of the Versailles box—'Jewel Yellow' and in front 'Sonora.' Also hosta 'Majesty' on the left. To the right in front: tree fern, the foliage of bleeding heart 'Gold Heart,' and *Choisya* 'Aztec Gold.'

It's a sport for me to find and put together plants that match each other. In fact, when I see a new plant that I haven't come across before, it immediately sets my thoughts in motion: In what context can I use it? What does it go with? There are so many exciting possibilities ...

A plant that I have had in the rotation for many years is the marigold 'Vanilla.' The name alone makes it hard to resist. I always have it in my planters under the kitchen windows. This year it was planted with white petunias, variegated ivy and the lime yellow *Helichrysum petiolare* 'Limelight.'

On the next page is the angel trumpet once again, and to its right a relatively new dahlia—'Platinum Blonde.' If you don't know, it can be hard to tell that it's a dahlia.

Bottom left is another plant of more recent date. It is *Cosmos bipinnatus* 'Xanthos.' When it appeared, many people's eyes widened a bit, because it was not a color previously seen in cosmos. It is fine, though not as strong as the others in the genus.

Bottom right is another dahlia. It's called 'Edna Comstock.'

Made for Each Other

It's as if white, yellow, and green are made for each other. Yellow can be tricky in some contexts, but here it's absolutely perfect. It may sound strange, but white—especially in large quantities—can also be hard to match with other colors. White can easily seem too chalky, too high-contrast.

For the first time this year I tried foxglove, *Digitalis*, in pots and it went quite well. In early spring we sowed the seeds, and in August the plants flowered. This may surprise some, as *Digitalis* is normally biennial and only flowers the year after sowing. But there is a series—'Camelot'—which flowers the same year it is sown. And it was one of these—'Camelot White'—that I tried. And as the picture on the far left shows, it turned out quite successfully.

The bush with the variegated leaves I came across by chance. Bluebeard, *Caryopteris* x *clandonensis* 'Summer Sorbet,' is the name. When it turns blue in late summer, I move it to another area of the garden. Low compact dahlias can be found anywhere. In the picture at the bottom left of the previous page it is 'Grande Lopez.' To the right is the winged *Nicotiana alata* 'Lime Green,' which we propagate from seed every year.

With their funnel-shaped flowers, lilies are useful in many contexts. The flower at the top right is not a lily in the usual sense. It is not a bulbous plant, but a perennial—the daylily, *Hemerocallis*. It blooms for a very long time, but as the common name suggests, each flower lasts only one day. This beautiful green-yellow variety is called 'Green Flutter.'

Earlier the cream-colored marigold 'Vanilla' appeared. At right is another fine variety—'Inca Yellowstones'—with almost greenish yellow flowers.

More Possibilities

On the previous pages I showed how I use white, cream, and yellow flowers together with lime-yellow and green foliage. On the following pages I will show you some examples of how nice the lime-colored foliage is also together with blue flowers. The large photo shows some different foliage and flowering plants. In the front row on the left is the lime yellow coralbell, *Heuchera* 'Lime Rickey.' Whether planted in a pot or bed, it can be difficult to overwinter. However, there is no problem with the lime-yellow growth with drooping vines on the right: the creeping Jenny, *Lysimachia nummularia* 'Aurea.'

Behind the Heuchera is *Coleus*, which is described in more detail on page 84. To the right is the mockorange, *Philadelphus coronaria* 'Aureus,' and at the back in front of the tree trunk is the ninebark, *Physocarpus opulifolius* 'Darts Gold.' The lush plant with blue flowers that weave into the surrounding growth is *Geranium* 'Rozanne.'

In the middle, below the blue flowers is the fan flower, *Scaevola*, see page 80. Far right is flossflower, *Ageratum houstonianum* 'Blue Horizon.'

Clear Favorites

There are plants that I love so much that they are permanent fixtures every year. One of them is the honeywort, *Cerinthe major* 'Purpurascens.' This is despite the fact that it is not very distinctive. But what the flowers don't have in size or glamour, they have in a subtle peculiarity that you don't see in any other flowers. With its blue-dusted flowers, it's simply something special. Although it looks a little delicate, it is exceptionally easy to deal with. The seeds, which are the size of peppercorns and completely black, can be sown directly in the pot: fill almost to the top with nutrient-enriched potting soil and finish with about 4 inches (10 cm) of additional potting soil.

The nasturtium, *Tropaeolum majus*, is one of the most common and easy summer flowers, good in beds as well as in pots. Here it can be sown directly as explained above by honeywort.

Years ago, it was mostly the orange-flowered varieties that were seen, but today there are so many different colors that it's quite a sight. One I'm particularly fond of is the creamy yellow 'Milkmaid.' It's so pretty alongside the blue flowers and lime foliage. I usually never use yellow flowers with yellowish foliage, but I'm making an exception here. That's because the solid yellow color that the nasturtiums contribute fits in so well. This is clear from the picture on pages 82–83.

On page 76 it is quite obvious what the cranesbill, *Geranium* 'Rozanne,' can do. I became acquainted with it at the beginning of my gardening career about twenty years ago, and now have several specimens in pots—just one plant in each. From here it spreads happily over the surrounding growth.

A Classic

When it comes to *Agapanthus*, I must say that I can't take my eyes off of huge plants with an impressive number of flowers. When I ask gardeners what they do to achieve this incredible flowering, they usually say that they don't really do anything except fertilize the plants.

I learn a lot when I travel. For example, a few years ago I visited an *Agapanthus* nursery in Holland. Here I was told that the most important thing is to keep fertilizing well into the autumn, because that's when the buds form. But it didn't work for me.

I think I'm on the right track anyway. When I was in Cornwall in the far southwest corner of England this summer, I saw wild *Agapanthus* everywhere. If they thrive so much in that place, it's because it has a subtropical climate with the Gulf Stream running past. And when a nurseryman told me that *Agapanthus* need sun, sun, and more sun, I realized not only do they need sun while they are flowering, but also afterward. And this is where I have failed. As soon as the flowers start to look sad, I usually move the plants to a secluded, shady spot backstage. This is, of course, really stupid, I now see. Next year, I promise, the plants will stay sunbaked well into autumn. It will be exciting.

Blue is Good

You can never go wrong with blue flowers. They fit in anywhere, and luckily there are plenty to choose from. Many are quite common, but I'll start with something of a rarity; that's *Salvia* 'Amistad.' It always attracts attention, and that's probably because the stems and the base of the flowers are almost black. Years ago I bought a plant in England and it has overwintered every year in the heated greenhouse. The thing is, *Salvia* 'Amistad' is not hardy. Over the years we have taken numerous cuttings, because it's a plant you can't have too many of.

Blue is a broad term in the plant world. Here, violet, purple, and lavender are all called blue. For example, see the dahlia at the top of the next page. At the bottom are a few other "blue" flowers. On the left is the fan flower, Scaevola. In the photo it may not look like much, but don't let that fool you. It is a very rich flowering plant. On the right is *Verbena* 'Lollipop.' It's pretty much identical to the well-known giant verbena, but only a bit lower—about 2 feet (60 cm).

Japanese sedge, *Carex oshimensis* 'Evergold,' goes so well with other lime-yellow foliage. As mentioned earlier, it is evergreen and therefore good for late summer and autumn groups.

Earlier I mentioned how garden visitors often notice the same plants. And they're certainly not always the most showy. This past season, for example, a lot of people wanted to know what the green poodle-like growth at the bottom was. I would have asked that too, because it's not exactly common in gardening. Actually, it's a houseplant called spikemoss, *Selaginella apoda*. I have planted four plants together in each pot, and when you know it, you can see it.

I am very fond of the flossflower, *Ageratum houstonianum* 'Blue Horizon,' seen at the top left of the next page. First of all because of its clear blue color, but also because it flowers right up to the arrival of frost. And it's easy to propagate from seed.

To the right is *Coleus* 'Electric Lime,' which lights up any setting. Coleus comes in many colors and has become immensely popular in recent years. In the past it was used exclusively as a pot plant.

Ninebark *Physocarpus opulifolius* 'Darts Gold,' bottom left has been mentioned before. It is an incredibly useful shrub that can be used anywhere. At the bottom you can also see the summer aster, *Callistephus chinensis* 'Tower Violet,' with its extremely intense color. It is propagated from seed and comes in many different colors. A really good pot plant.

Delicious Lime

My collection of lime-colored deciduous plants is expanding year by year, and new ones are being added all the time. Not so many years ago, a yellow variety of the well-known perennial called Japanese spikenard was introduced. It is called *Aralia cordata* 'Sun King' and is shown on the previous page on the left of the large group. Here it is a bit squashed, but in a bed it develops into a small shrub.

Between the two flossflowers stands a sweet potato, *Ipomoea batatas* 'Sweet Caroline Light Green.' It is not so well known and deserves more widespread use. On the top step is the almost lime-yellow spotted deadnettle, *Lamium maculatum* 'Aureum,' a perennial that turns pink when it's ready to bloom. Then we cut it all the way down. Partly to avoid the flowers and partly to achieve compact growth. On the far right of the picture is a bleeding heart, *Dicentra spectabilis* 'Gold Heart.' After flowering it was cut back completely and then sprouted with fresh lime yellow foliage. Last in the yellowish company is the plant with yellow-brown foliage behind the bleeding heart. It is a half-shrub—the wintercreeper *Euonymus fortunei* 'Emerald Gold.' The plant in the center below is bee balm, *Monarda* 'Blaustrumpf.'

Dahlias in Good Company

Dahlias, like roses, benefit from the right company. I don't like pure dahlias or rose beds without companion plants.

Before I get into the dahlias used here, I'll review the plants on the previous page. First, let me introduce the lime-yellow ones that really shine in this context. The two groups on the right are *Coleus* 'Lime Time.' Midway above the coleus is *Rubus cockburnianus* 'Goldenvale.' It weaves in with the surrounding plants. On the first step is the feverfew, *Tanacetum parthenium* 'Aureum.' The aromatic foliage smells of chamomile. Further up, on the second step, is the anise hyssop, *Agastache foeniculum* 'Golden Jubilee.' It has the most stunning lime-yellow foliage and is grown easily from seed.

Just to the right of the door is Texas sage, *Salvia farinacea* 'Midnight Candle,' with the deepest blue flowers. Below the anise hyssop, a spider flower, *Cleome* 'Señorita Rosalita,' peeks out. It is also the one seen at the bottom middle. Also dotted around is the low lavender phlox, *Phlox* 'Summerstars.' The grass-like growth seen in several places in the foreground is the great wood-rush, *Luzula sylvatica* 'Aurea.' In spring the foliage is a striking lime yellow.

Last but not least, the plant with the tall purple spires should be mentioned. Many people are surprised when they are told that it is a lobelia. But there are other kinds than the small-flowered ones for your balcony boxes. This one, called *Lobelia* 'Hadspen Purple,' is incomparable in both pots and garden beds. However, it is somewhat sensitive to winter cold.

The picture on the previous page clearly shows how the dahlias are good for creating height in the arrangement. In the foreground is the anise hyssop, *Agastache* 'Black Adder.'

It is so tempting to use many different dahlias because there are so many beautiful ones. But it creates more harmony to repeat two or three varieties. Here is the relatively new 'Blue Bayou' with 'Balthasar.' The latter can be recognized by its completely dark stems.

When the dahlias grow as tall as they do here, it's because they have something to live on. Dahlias are hungry plants!

The Lovely Dahlias

One of the plants that is absolutely indispensable in my pot gardens is the dahlia. From the end of July until well into October, we enjoy the impressive flowers this plant produces.

The popularity of dahlias is evident on social media. In fact, I would go so far as to say that they have never been more popular than they are today. The flowers are lovely in a vase, even if they don't last very long. But you just have to keep picking, because the more flowers you pick, the more you get. The trick is to stop the flowers from going to seed, because then the flowering stops.

There are a number of different flower shapes. The pompom form is the most popular of all, and within this group 'Stolze von Berlin' is a clear favorite. It is the one seen in the large photo. As you can see, it is a very rich flowering variety.

Below is the 'Park Princess.' It is a relatively new acquaintance, and one advantage of this variety is that it only grows about 2 feet (60 cm) tall.

Shocking Pink

Hot pink is a color that does really well in the company of other pinks. It's a little more cheeky and adds character to the often overly sweet look that pink flowers represent.

The range of pink flowers is large in both summer flowers, dahlias, roses, and perennials. The bright pink flowers are summer asters, *Callistephus chinensis* 'Duchess Coral,' grown from seed. There are many different varieties. This pairs so well with the garden phlox, *Phlox paniculata* 'Edentuin,' with a darker pink eye, standing in the background.

A favorite dahlia is 'Fascination,' seen top left on the next page. A classic variety with dark foliage, it grows to only about 40 inches (100 cm) tall.

I've never had much luck with roses in pots—at least not more than one season at a time. That's why we plant them out in the garden at the end of the season. The cute little rose on the right is called 'Cerisc Flower Circus.'

As you will see from the pictures on the next page, it is beautiful to combine pink and rose tones with gray foliage. For example blue fescue *Festuca glauca* 'Elijah Blue,' seen here in the bottom photo.

Pink and Gray …

… are two shades that go very well together. Earlier, it was shown how well gray foliage goes with white flowers, but in the company of pink flowers, the silvery foliage is also distinctive.

Above is the summer flower that tops them all: *Cosmos bipinnatus* 'Double Click Rose Bonbon.' The reason I like this cosmos so much is that it is easy to grow, has the loveliest flowers and foliage, and is so beautiful in both bed and pot.

Top left on the next page is Tibetan dewberry, *Rubus thibetanus* 'Silver Fern.' It produces shoots up to a meter and a half long, weaving in between surrounding plants.

The growth on the top right I want to emphasize because of the nice little pink flowers. Although they are quite discreet, you still notice them. The plant is smartweed, *Polygonum capitatum*, which can be grown from seed. If you can overwinter the plant frost-free, it is perennial. We overwinter a plant or two and take cuttings in the spring. It's quite easy.

The rose at the bottom is called 'Pompon Flower Circus.' It is easy to recognize with its greenish-pink flowers. The neighboring plant is *Heuchera* 'Peppermint Spice.' On the far right is October stonecrop, *Sedum sieboldii*.

Pure Romance

As you can see, the garden has many spaces, corners and nooks where I can work with different color schemes. So, when you step out of the greenhouse to the east, you come to this pink space.

My three greenhouses are not only practical for plant propagation, they also create a special atmosphere and act very much as room dividers, allowing potted plants to be arranged artfully.

The garden is just over 43,000 square feet (4,000 sq m), and although it is a relatively large garden, I think it has succeeded in creating an intimate universe. And for this the many pot arrangements are indispensable.

To present the plants beautifully, I designed and had display stairs made of galvanized iron and concrete tiles. The rough look was chosen as a counterpoint to the romantic flowers. To the right of the entrance, on the bottom shelf, is *Verbena* 'Homestead Pink' next to Mexican fleabane, *Erigeron karvinskianus* 'Profusion.' It is so adorable with its small bellis-like flowers, but unfortunately it is not hardy. We overwinter it in the heated greenhouse. Above the verbena is the spider flower, *Cleome* 'Señorita Mi Amor,' which flowers all summer.

On the next page are two indispensable plants, both of which can be sown from seed. Above is rose mallow, *Lavatera trimestris* 'Pink Beauty.' The funnel-shaped flowers look delicate. But don't let that fool you, because rose mallows are incredibly easy to grow and it only takes a couple of months for the first flowers to appear.

At the bottom is the flowering tobacco, *Nicotiana mutabilis*. It is remarkable in that the flowers change between white, rose, and pink. The plants grow to well over 3 feet (1 m) tall.

A New Display

Previous photos have shown how we decorate every spring with spring-blooming bulbs outside the gate down by the road. When the daffodils and tulips die down during May, they are removed and a new display is made. This one, with pink lupines as the absolute heroes, was seen by many passers-by in June. The varied exhibitions have become my calling card, showing a little of my skills. The gate is closed, but a few days a year I keep the garden open for Gold Members of Claus Dalby's Garden Club.

The pink lupine is called 'Blossom.' As with so many other special plants, it cannot be sown from seed, but must be propagated from cuttings. Unfortunately, it is rather short-lived. Here is 'Blossom' in the company of *Bellis* 'Strawberries and Cream,' which has exactly the same pink color. The other flowering plant with small white flowers is *Spiraea betulifolia* 'Tor Gold.' The plants with the large downy leaves are the silver sage, *Salvia argentea*, mentioned earlier. The low shrubs with variegated leaves are tatarian dogwood, *Cornus alba* 'Elegantissima.'

Finally, the wire-netting bush, *Corokia cotoneaster*, which is actually an indoor plant, but it thrives outdoors and even withstands a few frosts.

Welcome

There was once a common marketing slogan: Say it with flowers. The flowers on our main staircase certainly say "Welcome" to our guests. That's why we always decorate with pots. It used to be a white and gray theme. Now it's a pinkish-gray. Every year I choose a new color theme. These pictures were taken in September.

I've mentioned before the beautiful oxalis, *Trifolium repens*, which comes in many color variations. This one is called 'Leonore' and with its gray-green and purple tones it pairs perfectly with the coralbell, *Heuchera* 'Peppermint Spice,' seen opposite.

In late summer and autumn, impressive chrysanthemum balls with hundreds of flower buds lure visitors to the country's garden centers. They are very versatile and do well in company with other plants. The large photo on pages 108–109 shows how I have used large pink chrysanthemum balls as "islands" between, among others, the silver cushion bush, *Calocephalus brownii*, and heather in two shades. In addition, there were wire vines and ivy, as well as the plants mentioned below.

The meadow spikemoss, *Selaginella apoda*, seen at the top of the next page, is particularly good in this context because it brightens up the scene with its fresh green appearance.

In the center of the bottom picture is *Sedum* 'Blue Cushion,' which with its grayish appearance is a discreet companion, especially to the somewhat lighter gray cushion bush.

Rust or Apricot?

Decide for yourself ... This color is a bit hard to define. In any case, many fall for it. It's probably because it's a tone you don't see every day.

Buchanan's sedge, *Carex buchananii*, top left, fits in perfectly. However, it has never been a commercial success. That's probably because you'd think it had died out, but it's alive and well. Earlier I mentioned the lime-yellow ninebark, but here it's a coppery variety: *Physocarpus opulifolius* 'Lady in Red,' seen above.

On the next page top left is *Coleus* 'Campfire.' It is a variety that needs to be propagated by cuttings. To the right is a summer flower, grown from seed: foxtail, *Amaranthus* 'Hot Biscuits.' It too has a special color.

Once again it is a small-flowered rose in the Flower Circus series. This apricot rose is called 'Cream Flower Circus.'

Like *Heuchera*, *Heucherella* is available in the most beautiful colors, and at the bottom right is *Heucherella* 'Brass Lantern.'

Anise hyssop, *Agastache* 'Kudos Ambrosia,' is just one of many new varieties of the well-known plant, which has a fantastic fragrance. The orange/apricot/pink little flowers seen on the left fit in so beautifully.

As I said, there are many different nasturtium varieties. It is a really lovely flower that can be sown directly in pots. *Tropaeolum* 'Tip Top Alaska Salmon' is the name of the variety on the left.

In the picture on the right, dahlias are in the spotlight and if you look closely, you can see the rusty support stands in the front pots, which were introduced on page 16–17. In the front pot on the corner, it's the dahlia 'Orange Nugget' that doesn't get that tall. That's why it's good in the foreground. At the base it is another of many coralbells, *Heuchera*. Here the variety name is 'Amber Waves.' On the left is Buchanan's sedge, *Carex buchananii*. The cactus-shaped dahlia at the top of the picture is called 'Preference.'

The following pages show dahlias, perennials, summer flowers, and foliage that play out well with each other.

The pots are set up to the left of the pyramid-shaped greenhouse. Here we have a small terrace where the gardeners and I sit and have morning and lunch breaks when the weather is nice. We have a lovely view. And as you can see, it doesn't take much space to create a thriving lush garden.

Free Choice

When it comes to dahlias, there are so many to choose from. Never has the range been greater and never have so many new varieties been added.

The impressive flower above is the popular variety 'Cafe au Lait,' which you see everywhere, not least on social media. It's won the hearts of many not only for its delicate creamy hue, but also for its flower size. It's called a dinner plate dahlia, which means that the flower is the size of a dinner plate.

Among the many different varieties, the round pompom shape is undoubtedly the most popular. Looking at the flower, you can't help but be fascinated by its graceful structure. The coral-colored pompom dahlia at the top left of the next page is called 'Jowey Winnie.' On the right is the single-flowered 'Happy Single Kiss' and on the bottom left is 'Preference.' Finally, the lily 'Tiger Babies.'

If you get the dahlia bug, as mentioned before, there are so many shapes and colors to choose from. On the left are two other forms—the first is called anemone. This one is called 'Apricot Desire.' Another form is referred to as decorative. The variety name of the dahlia in the bottom photo is 'Jewel Salmon.'

Quite Exotic

Canna is a tuberous plant that is similar to dahlia in terms of cultivation. When I grow them, it is mainly because of the leaves. Some varieties have incredibly beautiful foliage, especially against the light.

One of my favorite varieties is 'B. Marley,' which has copper-colored foliage that appears striped when you see the leaf veins up against the sun.

If you want flowering, you need a warm summer or a greenhouse, as the canna is a heat-loving plant. 'B. Marley' produces orange flowers.

Canna tubers are planted at the same time as dahlia tubers, see pages 16–17. Here too, they should not be too deep.

Another exotic-looking specimen is the hibiscus, which does well here. There are several hardy hibiscus that can grow into large shrubs over the years. Unfortunately, we don't have quite enough sun for them to thrive here in the garden. They simply don't get to flower. So I "cheat" and get mature plants from a hibiscus breeder known for their large flowering potted plants. However, a beautiful variety with many smaller flowers stands out. It is 'Petit Orange,' which has won many awards.

Glowing Tones

There's a fine balance between apricot—as discussed in previous pages—and orange, as it applies now. It really is a color that, florally, people have embraced in the last few years.

The picture on this page is from late June, and as can be seen, the groups are not yet that developed. This is partly because the dahlias planted in the spring are not yet ready. They are still in storage.

The low dahlias I have not grown myself, but bought "ready." The fine variety with dark foliage and orange flowers is called 'Happy Days Neon.' The nasturtium on the right of the next page is called 'Vesuvius.' The others are 'Tip Top Alaska Salmon.'

On the next page it is clear that more plants have been added. We are now in the middle of August. Canna 'B. Marley' has already been described, but here is also a variety with completely dark leaves. It is called 'Black Knight' and has red flowers.

To the left of the tree trunk is a darkened bush. Once again it is the ninebark, *Physocarpus opulifolius*, and here it is the best known variety, 'Diabolo.' Like the other varieties, it produces white flowers, but because we prune the bushes every spring, no flowers appear. This is not a loss, because they just seem disruptive in this context.

To the right of the stool is another of the book's many coralbells: *Heuchera* 'Marmalade.'

Brown and Burnt

Some plants fall out of favor with gardeners. Among these are marigolds, but I'd like to do something about that. As I said, there are so many fine ones. Among them *Tagetes linnaeus*, seen on the left of the previous page. A beautiful selection with tall and slender stems. On the right is the orange pompom dahlia 'Bantling.'

Nemesia 'Sunsatia Blood Orange,' bottom left, is so intense in color that you can't help but notice it. Here it is in the company of *Heuchera* 'Sweet Tea.'

Bottom right is another notable performer, *Zinnia* 'Profusion Double Fire.' The 'Profusion' series, which includes a range of colors, is somewhat lower and bushier than the usual tall types. I love the tall ones, but have never had much luck with them in pots, unfortunately. I have, however, with 'Profusion.'

Another relatively low plant is the orange dahlia 'Gallery Cobra,' seen below. It only grows to about 12–14 inches (30–35 cm) tall.

A Trilogy

I've said it many times, but it can't be repeated too often: When putting together plants in general, and flowers in particular, it's not just about color, but very much about form. Especially if, as here, you arrange the plants in a monochromatic color scheme.

On the previous page at the top you see a very beautiful dahlia with the name 'Cornel Brons.' It has the shape of a pompom, but as the flower is quite large, it belongs to the group called *Ball*.

The cactus dahlias are not to be mistaken. Bottom left is 'Ludwig Helfert.' Sometimes you meet people who think cactus dahlias seem too artificial, but I don't want to do without them. Especially because they offer variety that is so important.

With its orange petals and purple center, the dahlia above is something special. It's called 'American Dawn.' I found it in Holland a few years ago. It was brand new then, but today it is possible to find it online.

It's About Nuances

When putting colors together, it's a delicate balance that determines whether the result will be sublime or a failure. It's hard to give a precise recipe; it depends on intuition.

Some flowers are multicolored, such as the dahlia 'Lady Jill' at the top left of the previous page. If you look at it, you can see dark red, violet, and apricot shades. If 'Lady Jill' is combined with flowers in one or more of these shades, an exciting look can be achieved. Notice it in combination with the apricot-colored pot marigold *Calendula* 'Apricot Pygmy' to the right. Now the apricot tone of the dahlia becomes extra apparent. It's an exciting game to try to make flowers take on colors that echo their neighbors.

At first glance, the orange dahlia 'Color Spectacle' at the bottom of the previous page will look orange. But hold it up against the calendula above and a hint of apricot reveals itself in the flower.

Speaking of calendula, on the right is 'Dandy'—a beautiful classic variety. Calendula are one of the easiest flowers to grow from seed, and the simplest way is to sow the seeds directly in the pot.

One plant you don't see much of these days is *Begonia*, but I have an idea that it's on its way back. At least varieties with small flowers and dark foliage like the one seen in the bottom photo. It's called 'Glowing Embers.' I was really pleasantly surprised by how profusely it flowered throughout the summer.

Next year I will try to order some tubers of different species and varieties to see how they behave.

New and Old

It's exciting to keep up to date with what's new in the plant world, but it mustn't be at the expense of the old familiar and safe plants. After all, the new plants are not always better than the old ones. That's why we sometimes see our long-time favorites disappear from the market.

A new marigold—at least for me—is called 'Strawberry Blonde,' see picture top left of previous page. Its flowers change from rusty red to apricot, and it is quite low and really nice in pots.

Dark foliage is always a big hit, and in dahlias, for example, it's something breeders aim for in new varieties. The dahlia 'David Howard,' seen top right on the previous page, is however an old classic that never goes out of fashion. It has beautiful orange flowers that become extra intense in color when compared to the dark leaves.

Korean perilla, *Perilla frutescens*, is a dark-leaved plant with beautifully serrated foliage that I grow solely for its leaves. It is also called Japanese shiso because it is used in Japanese cuisine. Not a novelty, but people notice it in the garden anyway.

Another plant that also attracts attention is the signet marigold, *Tagetes tenuifolia*. It has small flowers that smell of orange. We sow the seeds directly in the pot.

The tall varieties of *Zinnia* can be a bit tricky, at least in pots. Top right is—for me—a new variety: 'Magellan Orange,' which is quite easy to grow.

Finally another classic dahlia with dark foliage and red flowers. It is called 'Ellen Houston' and grows no more than 20–40 inches (50–60 cm) tall.

A Fireworks Display

In the introduction I told you how to combine colors like pink, purple, orange, blue, violet and lime. This range of tones can be attributed to one person in particular—fashion designer Kenzo Takada, who was born in Japan in 1939. He later moved to France and opened his own fashion house, which soon became known for its use of these strong colors.

When guests arrive in the garden, they are first introduced to the large English-inspired garden in front of the house. It consists of a series of hedged rooms with flowers and plants In predominantly white and muted tones, where the atmosphere is romantic. At this point, guests have only seen the potted plants outside the gate. My idea is that little by little, visitors will be exposed to various surprises. What's around the next corner? Because a garden should not be observed from one place. It must always offer something new.

Then, as they come around the greenhouse, the first of the garden's pots reveal themselves, and then they come to The Sunken Garden. From here, they pass the Victorian greenhouse and make their way to the square in front of the pyramid-shaped greenhouse.

On the tour, guests are constantly exposed to new color combinations. It's a bit like eating your way through a menu of varying flavors.

Meeting this color bombardment, where the plants mingle and form an impressive whole, I have often seen people start to smile.

The pyramid-shaped greenhouse was completed just four years ago. For the first several years there was a parking lot here, but one day I suddenly had a vision. Why hadn't I thought of it before? It was the perfect place for a greenhouse. The idea was born in late summer, and by early spring the greenhouse was ready. I was happy for the new covered growing space, but also for the space created around it. It really has become a playground where I can let off steam.

Greenhouse and square designed by Kjeld Slot.

To Paint with Flowers

I've always had a creative mind, but I've never been able to draw or paint in the usual sense. Nevertheless, I would say that my sense of color is quite well developed. I think in colors and am quite good at remembering different tones. This comes in handy when I see new flowers and plants. Then it doesn't take me long to figure out which company they'll fit in with.

When we took over this place, there was no garden. The canvas was blank, so to speak, so now I could start painting—with plants…

Above is one of my motifs. Here it is on top, the snapdragon, *Antirrhinum* 'Pretty in Pink.' At the bottom is the flowering tobacco, *Nicotiana alata* 'Lime Green,' which with its lime green flowers fits into any setting. In the middle, yarrow, *Achillea millefolium* 'Walther Funcke,' attracts attention.

Finally *Agapanthus*, whose flowers stick out behind the flowering tobacco.

On the next page are a small handful of plants that would be perfect for the party: dahlia 'Ambition,' hydrangea 'Little Lime,' *Calibrachoa* 'Callie Orange,' and an unnamed dahlia seedling.

Seeing Red

As I sat and pondered how to begin this section, I found a quote:

Red is associated with blood, heart, life, passion, strong emotions, heat, fire, sacrifice and danger. Red stands for aggressiveness and vitality. It is the color of love, but also of hate and rage. Red is the color of battle, of war and therefore of the military. The Romans used red as a symbol of power, the emperor, the nobility and the warriors. The color is associated with Mars, the god of war. It can symbolize revolution, socialism, communism (red flags).

No other color seems to evoke so many associations. That's why red is such an inspiring color to work with. There are several tones, and many people love the deep dark red flowers. This applies to tulips, roses, and dahlias, for example. Plants with dark foliage are also popular. It can be tempting to put a lot of dark flowers together, but be aware that it can easily become too gloomy. However, with high red and also preferably orange, a completely different impression is achieved, as shown in the picture on the left. In this context, gray foliage is also very nice.

The long red bed behind the Victorian greenhouse is made up of summer flowers, perennials, and especially dahlias. On the next pages I will talk about some of the plants. Let me start with some good summer flowers, sown from seed:

Top right is the foxtail, *Amaranthus cruentus* 'Hopi Red Dye,' with nice dark foliage. The bottom photo shows *Rudbeckia hirta* 'Cherry Brandy' with the most beautiful velvety red flowers. The neighboring plant, *Daucus carota* 'Dara,' on the next page.

A very special foliage plant that everyone notices is the multicolored Japanese painted fern, *Athyrium niponicum* 'Pictum,' seen above left. With its reddish veins and grayish foliage, it fits so well into this context. On the right is *Sedum* 'Purple Emperor' with the most delicate dark foliage. In late summer red flowers burst forth. The red foliage is from the Japanese maple, *Acer japonicum* 'Beni Maiko.'

At the top of the next page is a well-known and much-loved plant. The dark flowers belong to the chocolate flower, *Cosmos atrosanguineus*. The plant got its common name because in warm weather the flowers smell of chocolate. But you have to stick your nose right down to them. The chocolate flower can be overwintered, but it does not tolerate frost. Throughout the winter, keep the soil evenly moist, but do not overwater the plant either.

The red-leaved fleece flower, *Persicaria microcephala* 'Red Dragon,' bottom left has been shown before. But it is so beautiful that it easily bears repeating.

A fairly new summer flower is the purple wild carrot, *Daucus carota* 'Dara,' seen bottom right. It's great, also in bouquets. We sprinkle the seeds over the mulch in the pot in April/May, and the rest takes care of itself.

With its brilliant red color, the 'Ruby Flower Circus' rose lights up between all the dark foliage. It is good in a pot throughout a single season. Then it moves out into the garden. As it's not that big a rose, I usually plant three together in the bed about a foot apart. Then in a few years they form a neat little dense bush.

Tradescantia pallida on the right is just one of many plants with dark foliage. Its fleshy and lanceolate leaves are not found in other plants. In more southerly climes it is often seen growing in the open. At home it must be overwintered frost-free.

Rex begonia, *Begonia rex* is one of those plants that has a wide range of uses. 'Casey Corwin' is the name of the variety on the bottom left. Next to it is the turbaned lily 'Red Life,' which I have had for many years.

Below is another fleece flower: *Persicaria microcephala* 'Purple Fantasy.' It only grows about 1½ feet (half a meter) tall and has small white flowers, but it's the foliage that's the attraction.

Red Dahlias

A browse through the book will show that I use dahlias in a great many contexts. I don't know what I would do without them from early to late summer when the large and colorful flowers start to pop out. They really "do" something.

On this page, I present a few of the many red varieties—from lipstick red to the very dark.

Above is an old favorite—'Bishop of Llandaff'—with dark foliage and bright red, simple flowers. It may not be a variety you fall for at first, but I'd hate to be without it, as it provides a necessary counterpoint to the very dark flowers such as 'Arabian Night,' seen top left on the next page.

Pompom-shaped dahlias are among the most popular, and within that group 'Ivanetti' at the top right of the next page is a clear favorite.

'Rip City' is a beautiful variety belonging to the group called semicactus—see picture bottom left on next page.

To the right is the 'Bishop of Auckland' with dark foliage and almost velvety, simple flowers.

Change Day

The display on page 104 lasted a good month. Then the lupines succumbed and, as they were the main attraction, it was time to change and create a new exhibition. No problem, there were plenty of plants in stock.

The only plants that were allowed to remain were silver sage, *Salvia argentea*, and wire-netting bush, *Corokia cotoneaster*. Partly because they only get more beautiful and fuller over the season, and partly because they fit in perfectly with the new arrangement the gardeners had devised. In fact, it was my talented gardeners who created this display. I am proud to have such talented staff. It is a great pleasure every day and I never have to worry about the well-being of the garden.

Birthe, Mariann, and Preben have been here for a number of years, and they know how I like it. I'm not a trained gardener, which is perhaps why I've developed my own style. It's a great pleasure to pass it on to them and to everyone who follows my activities in TV programs, books, articles, and on social media.

At the top left is the basil 'Magic Mountain.' It is somewhat coarser than the common types and is more for ornamental than culinary use. The plants can be overwintered at temperatures above 54°F (12°C). To the right is the flowering tobacco *Nicotiana alata* 'Perfume Purple.' It is a must in my pots every year because of its almost velvety surface and deep purple color.

On the far left of the picture on page 150 is the low dahlia 'Happy Days Purple.' It's found in several places throughout the garden. The purple plant behind the low dahlia is spider flower, *Cleome* 'Señorita Rosalita.'

Around it are several dark-leaved plants without flowers. This is red orache, *Atriplex hortensis rubra*, which is an unusually easy plant. Midway and at the top are some dahlia flowers that unmistakably look like 'Happy Days Purple.' But these plants are somewhat taller. Here is the variety name 'Happy Single Wink.'

And in the foreground is the little oxalis, *Trifolium repens* 'Isabella.'

September Flower

The arrangement on the previous pages lasted a few months. Only in September was it time for a refresh, and some new plants were added. Only a few of the original ones were replaced: dahlia 'Happy Days Purple' and red orache, *Atriplex hortensis rubra*. The rest were rotated around and were joined by, among others, new medium height dahlias that I had bought "ready" at flowering: the purple one, which appears at the top left in the photo at left, is called 'Castilla,' and the bright pink one 'Salinas.' The top left picture on the next page shows 'Cadena,' and the picture on the right shows 'Happy Single Wink.'

New arrivals in the photo on the left include red cabbage plants, which with their blue-dusted leaves fit in perfectly. *Verbena* 'Lollipop,' also seen in the bottom photo, has also been added. As I said, it looks like a giant verbena, but at around 2 feet (60 cm) it is somewhat shorter.

I like for people to smile when they pass the plant arrangements outside the gate. That's why it's fun to complement with cabbage plants, for example—both red cabbage and red kale, shown in the top left photo on the next page. The crinkled leaves create an interesting variation. Behind the cabbage is *Sedum cauticola* with pink flowers. Before the flowers burst out, it is the grayish purple tone of the foliage that attracts attention.

In addition, kohlrabi has been used, which can be seen in the picture at the bottom of the next page. Both the color of the kohlrabi bulb itself and its leaves match this composition perfectly. The leaf veins are violet, while the leaves are otherwise gray, like the silver sage.

Big Moving Day

At the beginning of October, the gardeners thought it was time for something new to happen. Now it was time for heather, and it was the only evergreen plant that got a place. The rest were deciduous.

This is the first time we have worked so intensively and so far into the year with our pottery arrangements. But it was my wish to present as many different ideas as possible in this book. And it's really inspiring to be able to show that the calendar doesn't put a limit on the lushness. Fortunately, we live in a mild place, where frost doesn't set in until quite late.

All the dahlias had done what they could for this year, but kale, kohlrabi, wire-netting bush, and oxalis escaped being removed. And once again it was the gardeners who arranged and composed. I've learned over time that I don't have to interfere in everything! However, I am the one who chooses and buys the plants, so there is something to play with.

There's not much green, but what there is, lights up well. On the far left is a pot that looks like it's boiling over. The green growth is a plant called brass buttons, *Cotula minima*. Behind it is a plant with green leaves and brown markings. It is the fleece flower, *Persicaria filiformis*. At the top, to the left of the wire-netting bush, is another fleece flower. It has red-brown foliage and is called *Persicaria microcephala* 'Red Dragon.' To prevent the two willows from growing too tall and falling over, we cut them down to the ground in early May. Then they grow again, become even denser and not so tall.

Grasses are part of the season, and in the middle you can see red-leaved fountain grass, *Pennisetum setaceum* 'Rubrum.' On the far right is *Pennisetum setaceum* 'Fireworks.' *Heuchera*, a coralbell, is seen in many places in the book, and here it is the very dark 'Obsidian' and the green-leaved with red veins, 'Peppermint Spice.' On the far left, next to the tree fern, is the rust-colored *Sedum* 'Chocolate Ball.' In the middle, with small, variegated leaves, is *Lophomyrtus × ralphii* 'Magic Dragon.' Finally, the rex begonia, *Begonia rex*. Its beautiful foliage can be seen in the photos above. The plant on the left is called 'Casey Corwin,' and the one on the right 'Helen Teupel.'

Nearing the Finale

Then the growing season was coming to its conclusion. At the end of October, we organized the last pot exhibition of the year at the gate. Compared to the display on the previous pages, the appearance changed a lot, despite the fact that several of our old acquaintances remained.

Here it is clear that both the cushion bush, *Calocephalus brownii*, and the gray pumpkins are lit up. The latter I bought in a farm shop, but you can also grow them yourself. This variety is called *Cucurbita maxima* 'Crown Prince.' Another growth that fits the party perfectly is *Senecio candicens* 'Angel Wings,' which was introduced earlier. With its almost white leaves it attracts justified attention.

Herbs are also good in many contexts, and here are thyme and sage, both of which have grayish foliage. And also rosemary.

We chose the pumpkin theme for Halloween, when we light candles and let them burn until dawn. See the picture on pages 160–161.

All Saints' Day or Halloween?

All Saints' Day is a Christian celebration in which people remember their dead in churches on the first Sunday in November. Halloween is the American version of All Saints' Day, with the religious content removed. Nowadays, Halloween is associated with horror because it is based on the old folk belief that on this night there was a particularly high risk of the dead returning to haunt the living. So people dress up in macabre costumes and light spooky pumpkin lanterns to scare away the spirits of the dead.

I don't like Jack o' lanterns very much. Instead, I decorate with whole orange pumpkins, which act as color bombs between all the foliage.

Once again I have chosen to let chrysanthemums play the leading role together with *Skimmia japonica* 'Rubella'—a very decorative evergreen shrub. As I said, there is a green variety, and in the picture on the next page you can see a copper-colored black one on the far right. It is called *Skimmia japonica* 'Brocox Rocker'

Drooping laurel, *Leucothoe walteri* 'Rainbow,' is an evergreen shrub. In late summer the foliage starts to turn rusty red, which makes it very useful here. It is seen on the far left and middle.

I'm always on the lookout for plants with special foliage that might fit into a particular design. Foliage plants are absolutely indispensable and a fantastic link between the flowering plants. The icing between the cake layers, so to speak. *Heuchera* is also important here. Three different varieties: on the far left is 'Sweet Tea,' middle 'Marmalade,' and down in front 'Peppermint Spice.'

Around it you can also see wintergreen, *Gaultheria miqueliana*, and *Sedum* 'Chocolate Ball.' In addition, there is Christmas rose, *Helleborus niger*, as well as rosemary and red fountain grass, *Pennisetum setaceum*.

The next image shows how the set up is decorated with candles.

November Flowering

It's amazing that some plants bloom right into the penultimate month of the year. But they do exist, and of course I take advantage of them.

Many of the deciduous plants are recurrents that have stood the distance throughout the season. These include ivy, wire vine, Christmas rose, and *Sedum*.

To create color, I have planted decorative cabbages in shades of violet and white. They only get prettier as the temperature drops. The colder it gets, the more intense the colors.

You can grow ornamental cabbage yourself, but I haven't had much luck. Fortunately, cabbages can be bought in late summer at most nurseries. It seems like ornamental cabbages have been a bit out of the picture in recent years, but I've always liked them. So I hope this book will help show how useful they are.

For this arrangement I have used two different plants in a few color variations. They are asters and harvest saxifrage, *Saxifraga cortusifolia*—a refined series consisting of a number of different varieties. Above are two—one pink and one white. They are called 'Autumn Grace Kumiko' and 'Autumn Grace Miharu' respectively.

Both pictures show 'Kumiko' with beautiful star-shaped pink flowers. It is so pretty. And remember, it's a perennial that can be planted out in the garden. Then it will come back year after year.

The bottom picture on the previous page shows the white aster 'Mystery Lady Jessica.' Above is the pink 'Mystery Lady Sasha.' I have chosen these two because they go perfectly with the ornamental cabbages.

If it doesn't freeze and it isn't too rainy, the flowers here can last a few weeks. Usually until Christmas decorating begins in late November.

Goodbye and Thanks

At the end of November, the pots are packed away. Then we decorate for Christmas and start preparing for a new season. Spring bulbs are planted and waiting in pots, seeds have been harvested, and the heat is on in the greenhouses.

Now it's time for *armchair gardening* ... I love it. Now to study the books I bought during the year and the magazines I didn't have time to flip through. Throughout the year, I've been writing notes about seeds and plants to include in the new season, and between Christmas and New Year, I'm getting on board with the seed catalogs. So the new season is slowly getting underway.

For people who are not so interested in gardens, it can be difficult to understand what we are doing. From early spring we work on building up and then at the end of the season we break down again. What's it all about? I can only answer for myself—in a busy day I need the cycle of gardening and nature. You could call it a form of therapy.

It makes me happy and proud. With this book, I hope to have passed on a little bit of my great passion.

Have a great time in your own garden.

Index